THE OFF...
KNOCK! KNOCK!
JOKE BOOK

written by:
Chris Tait

kidsbooks Incorporated

Copyright © 2000 Kidsbooks Inc.
3535 West Peterson Avenue
Chicago, IL 60659

All rights reserved including the right of
reproduction in whole or in part in any form.

Manufactured in Canada

Visit us at: www.kidsbooks.com
Volume discounts available for group purchases.

If you're nutty for knock-knock jokes, then this is the book for you! *The Official Knock! Knock! Joke Book* is jam-packed with jokes that will have you and your pals rolling in the aisles. From the old favorites that everyone knows, to new knock-knock humor you've probably never heard, we've got it all waiting for you right here.

Knock, Knock!
Who's there?
Ben.
Ben who?
Ben a long time since I've seen you!

Knock, Knock!
Who's there?
Don.
Don who?
Don tell me you don't
remember me?

Knock, Knock!
Who's there?
Ax.
Ax who?
Ax nicely, and I might tell you!

Knock, Knock!
Who's there?
Arnold.
Arnold who?
Arnold friend from far away!

Knock, Knock!
Who's there?
Osborn!
Osborn who?
Osborn today!
That makes it my birthday!

Knock, Knock!
Who's there?
House!
House who?
House about you let me come inside!

Knock, Knock!
Who's there?
Isaiah!
Isaiah who?
Isaiah nothing else until
you let me in!

Knock, Knock!
Who's there?
Chester!
Chester who?
Chester luck, you forgot
my name again!

Knock, Knock!
Who's there?
Betty!
Betty who?
Betty doesn't even know
his own name!

Knock, Knock!
Who's there?
Sultan!
Sultan who?
Sultan pepper makes everything
taste better!

Knock, Knock!
Who's there?
Chuck!
Chuck who?
Chuck and see if you recognize me!

Knock, Knock!
Who's there?
Leggo!
Leggo who?
Leggo of me and I'll tell you!

Knock, Knock!
Who's there?
Gino!
Gino who?
Gino who it is,
I'm your twin brother!

Knock, Knock!
Who's there?
Phil!
Phil who?
Phil my drink for me, will you?

Knock, Knock!
Who's there?
Isis!
Isis who?
Isis giving me a headache!

Knock, Knock!
Who's there?
Dennis!
Dennis who?
Dennis is my favorite game!

Knock, Knock!
Who's there?
Senior!
Senior who?
Senior so nosey, I'm not going to
tell you who it is!

Knock, Knock!
Who's there?
Iguana!
Iguana who?
Iguana hold your hand!

Knock, Knock!
Who's there?
Lion!
Lion who?
Lion down on the job
will get you fired!

Knock, Knock!
Who's there?
Hayden!
Hayden who?
Hayden won't do any good, I can
see you through the mail slot!

Knock, Knock!
Who's there?
Burton!
Burton who?
Burton me are going fishing,
want to come?

Knock, Knock!
Who's there?
Leaf!
Leaf who?
Leaf me alone with all
your silly questions!

Knock, Knock!
Who's there?
Izzy!
Izzy who?
Izzy coming out to play, or do I have to stand here all day?

Knock, Knock!
Who's there?
Cello!
Cello who?
Cello there, my little friend. How are you?

Knock, Knock!
Who's there?
Sara!
Sara who?
Sara nother question you could ask me other than who?

Knock, Knock!
Who's there?
Ken!
Ken who?
Ken I come in, or are you gonna
leave me out here all day?

Knock, Knock!
Who's there?
Ollie!
Ollie who?
Ollie said was that I should
come visit you!

Knock, Knock!
Who's there?
Don Juan!
Don Juan who?
Don Juan to go to school today.
It's too nice outside!

Knock, Knock!
Who's there?
Lisa!
Lisa who?
Lisa you can do is let me in!
It's pouring rain!

Knock, Knock!
Who's there?
Rufus!
Rufus who?
Rufus leaking; you better
get it fixed!

Knock, Knock!
Who's there?
Simon!
Simon who?
Simon the other side of the door.
If you opened it, you'd know!

Knock, Knock!
Who's there?
Shane!
Shane who?
Shane on you! You don't
recognize your own brother!

Knock, Knock!
Who's there?
Kenneth!
Kenneth who?
Kenneth kids come inthide?

Knock, Knock!
Who's there?
Wade!
Wade who?
Wade till I get inside,
then I'll tell you!

Knock, Knock!
Who's there?
Alfie!
Alfie who?
Alfie crying out loud,
stop asking!

Knock, Knock!
Who's there?
Tex!
Tex who?
Tex one to know one!

Knock, Knock!
Who's there?
Little old lady!
Little old lady who?
I didn't know you could yodel!
Do you sing too?

Knock, Knock!
Who's there?
Cassidy!
Cassidy who?
Cassidy was going to be right back.
Is he home?

Knock, Knock!
Who's there?
Sam!
Sam who?
Sam day, you'll remember.
Then you'll feel silly!

Knock, Knock!
Who's there?
Zoe!
Zoe who?
Zoe doesn't recognize
my voice now?

Knock, Knock!
Who's there?
Colleen!
Colleen who?
Colleen all cars. Colleen all cars!
We have a knock-knock joke in
progress!

Knock, Knock!
Who's there?
Mabel!
Mabel who?
Mabel syrup is good on waffles!

Knock, Knock!
Who's there?
Yuri!
Yuri who?
Yuri up and open the door!

Knock, Knock!
Who's there?
Ach!
Ach who?
Gesundheit!

Knock, Knock!
Who's there?
Maya!
Maya who?
Maya foot seems to be a
caught in your door!

Knock, Knock!
Who's there?
Klaus!
Klaus who?
Klaus the window, I can hear
your television all the way
down the street!

Knock, Knock!
Who's there?
Thermos!
Thermos who?
Thermos be some way out of here!

Knock, Knock!
Who's there?
Deecha!
Deecha who?
Deecha miss me while I was gone?

Knock, Knock!
Who's there?
Sandy!
Sandy who?
Sandy beaches beat
snowstorms any day!

Knock, Knock!
Who's there?
Boo!
Boo who?
There, there, don't cry.
It'll be okay!

Knock, Knock!
Who's there?
Mary!
Mary who?
Mary me, why don't ya?

Knock, Knock!
Who's there?
Max!
Max who?
Max no difference if you let me in
or not! I can wait all day!

Knock, Knock!
Who's there?
Paul!
Paul who?
Paul up a chair, and I'll tell you!

Knock, Knock!
Who's there?
Sweden!
Sweden who?
Sweden sour chicken is yummy!

Knock, Knock!
Who's there?
Augusta!
Augusta who?
Augusta wind is coming your way!

Knock, Knock!
Who's there?
Daryl!
Daryl who?
Daryl never be another
girl like you!

Knock, Knock!
Who's there?
Tom Sawyer!
Tom Sawyer who?
Tom Sawyer paint job on his fence.
Boy are you in trouble!

Knock, Knock!
Who's there?
Simon!
Simon who?
Simon the dotted line and all your
troubles will be over!

Knock, Knock!
Who's there?
Water!
Water who?
Water you waiting for?
Open up!

Knock, Knock!
Who's there?
Tony!
Tony who?
Tony even know me anymore, eh?
That's not very nice!

Knock, Knock!
Who's there?
Ping Pong!
Ping Pong who?
Ping Pong, the bells are ringing!

Knock, Knock!
Who's there?
Noah!
Noah who?
Noah don't recognize your voice
either! How strange!

Knock, Knock!
Who's there?
Sammy
Sammy who?
Sammy the check in the mail!

Knock, Knock!
Who's there?
Tyson!
Tyson who?
Tyson sugar on your cereal.
It's good!

Knock, Knock!
Who's there?
Deluxe!
Deluxe who?
Deluxe Ness Monster!

Knock, Knock!
Who's there?
Barry!
Barry who?
Barry happy to meet you!

Knock, Knock!
Who's there?
Felix!
Felix who?
Felix me again, I'm never petting
your dog again!

Knock, Knock!
Who's there?
Kerry!
Kerry who?
Kerry me upstairs, would you?
I'm pooped!

Knock, Knock!
Who's there?
Manny!
Manny who?
Manny needs a bath,
have you smelled him?

Knock, Knock!
Who's there?
Ember!
Ember who?
Ember me? I'm your best friend!

Knock, Knock!
Who's there?
Fletcher!
Fletcher who?
Fletcher self relax a little. Let go
every once in a while!

Knock, Knock!
Who's there?
Francis!
Francis who?
Francis hello and wants to know
what you're doing later.

Knock, Knock!
Who's there?
You!
You who?
Yes, how can I help you?

Knock, Knock!
Who's there?
Liam!
Liam who?
Liam where he is. If he wants to
come, he'll come!

Knock, Knock!
Who's there?
Les!
Les who?
Les go swimming while
it's still sunny!

Knock, Knock!
Who's there?
Fred!
Fred who?
Fred sox are my favorite team!

Knock, Knock!
Who's there?
Fuschia!
Fuschia who?
Fuschia the door on me one more
time, that's it!

Knock, Knock!
Who's there?
Vaughan!
Vaughan who?
Vaughan day you'll stop
acting so crazy!

Knock, Knock!
Who's there?
Pickle!
Pickle who?
Pickle lily and give it
to your mother!

Knock, Knock!
Who's there?
Theodore!
Theodore who?
Theodore is locked! Come in this
one instead.

Knock, Knock!
Who's there?
Gerald!
Gerald who?
Gerald if you can't see me
from this close!

Knock, Knock!
Who's there?
Ivana!
Ivana who?
Ivana suck your blood!

Knock, Knock!
Who's there?
Claire!
Claire who?
Claire the way! I'm coming through!

Knock, Knock!
Who's there?
Kenny!
Kenny who?
Kenny let me in or what?

Knock, Knock!
Who's there?
Annie!
Annie who?
Annie body home?

Knock, Knock!
Who's there?
Christine!
Christine who?
Christine that you don't live here
anymore, but I told him you did!

Knock, Knock!
Who's there?
Cook!
Cook who?
You're the one who's cuckoo!

Knock, Knock!
Who's there?
Falafel!
Falafel who?
Falafel my skateboard and
landed on my knee!

Knock, Knock!
Who's there?
Island!
Island who?
Island on my feet when I jump!

Knock, Knock!
Who's there?
Luck!
Luck who?
Luck through the keyhole!

Knock, Knock!
Who's there?
Tarzan!
Tarzan who?
Tarzan stripes forever!

Knock, Knock!
Who's there?
Althea!
Althea who?
Althea later alligathor!

Knock, Knock!
Who's there?
Scotland!
Scotland who?
Scotland on his head. We're gonna
have to take him to the hospital!

Knock, Knock!
Who's there!
Irish!
Irish who?
Irish you'd take me to
the soccer game!

Knock, Knock!
Who's there?
Wales!
Wales who?
Wales long as I'm here,
why don't we go out?

Knock, Knock!
Who's there?
Giovanni!
Giovanni who?
Giovanni go to the park with me?

Knock, Knock!
Who's there?
Justin!
Justin who?
Justin time for dinner!

Knock, Knock!
Who's there?
Marcus!
Marcus who?
Marcus down for two tickets. We're going to the show!

Knock, Knock!
Who's there?
Hey Alex!
Hey Alex who?
Hey, Alex the questions around here!

Knock, Knock!
Who's there?
Larry!
Larry who?
Larry funny, now open the door!

Knock, Knock!
Who's there?
Otto!
Otto who?
Otto be a law against knock-knock
jokes like these!

Knock, Knock!
Who's there?
Treachers!
Treachers who?
Treachers for you if you can guess!

Knock, Knock!
Who's there?
Homie!
Homie who?
Homie where the heart is!

Knock, Knock!
Who's there?
Vanessa!
Vanessa who?
Vanessa good time to come back?

Knock, Knock!
Who's there?
Amy!
Amy who?
Amy day now you could
let me inside.

Knock, Knock!
Who's there?
Wendy!
Wendy who?
Wendy clock strikes twelve,
it's lunch time!

Knock, Knock!
Who's there?
Daniella!
Daniella who?
Daniella so loud! I can hear
you just fine.

Knock, Knock!
Who's there?
Holden!
Holden who?
Holden, I'll go see!

Knock, Knock!
Who's there?
Yuni!
Yuni who?
Yuni to keep reading these
knock-knock jokes!

Knock, Knock!
Who's there?
Benny!
Benny who?
Benny where interesting lately?

Knock, Knock!
Who's there?
Who?
Who who?
I didn't know you were an owl!

Knock, Knock!
Who's there?
Freddie!
Freddie who?
Freddie or not, here I come!

Knock, Knock!
Who's there?
Jess!
Jess who?
Hey, that's my line!

Knock, Knock!
Who's there?
Jimmy!
Jimmy who?
Jimmy back my book, you thief!

Knock, Knock!
Who's there?
Cocoa!
Cocoa who?
Cocoa nuts are for monkeys,
not people!

Knock, Knock!
Who's there?
Tailor!
Tailor who?
Tailor head, your choice!

Knock, Knock!
Who's there?
Tina!
Tina who?
Tina little bug just bit me
right on the nose!

Knock, Knock!
Who's there?
Joanna!
Joanna who?
Joanna big kiss or what?

Knock, Knock!
Who's there?
Anne Maureen!
Anne Maureen who?
Anne Maureen the lawn,
I'll talk to you later!

Knock, Knock!
Who's there?
Roger!
Roger who?
Roger be talking to someone
who knew me!

Knock, Knock!
Who's there?
Jo!
Jo who?
Jo team Jo!

Knock, Knock!
Who's there?
Juan!
Juan who?
Juan hear some more
knock-knock jokes?

Knock, Knock!
Who's there?
Eddy!
Eddy who?
Eddy idea how I can get rid
ub dis cold?

Knock, Knock!
Who's there?
Cathy!
Cathy who?
Cathy crook before he geths away!

Knock, Knock!
Who's there?
Copperfield!
Copperfield who?
Copperfield bad so I came instead!

Knock, Knock!
Who's there?
Frank Lee!
Frank Lee who?
Frank Lee my dear,
I don't give a darn!

Knock, Knock!
Who's there?
Suzy!
Suzy who?
Suzy opens the door, grab him!

Knock, Knock!
Who's there?
Joey!
Joey who?
Joey to the world! It's Christmas!

Knock, Knock!
Who's there?
Rain!
Rain who?
Rain deer, you remember me, the one with the shiny, red nose?

Knock, Knock!
Who's there?
Snow!
Snow who?
Snow way I'm going out there, it's freezing!

Knock, Knock!
Who's there?
Harold!
Harold who?
Harold are you anyway?

Knock, Knock!
Who's there?
Everest!
Everest who?
Everest your eyes during the middle
of class? The teacher hates that!

Knock, Knock!
Who's there?
Penny!
Penny who?
Penny for your thoughts!

Knock, Knock!
Who's there?
Agatha!
Agatha Who?
Agatha sore tooth!   It's killing me!

Knock, Knock!
Who's there?
Harry!
Harry Who?
Harry up and take me to the dentist!

Knock, Knock!
Who's there?
Ollie!
Ollie Who?
Ollie want for Christmas is
my two front teeth!

Knock, Knock!
Who's there?
Becka!
Becka who?
Becka the bus is the
best place to sit!

Knock, Knock!
Who's there?
Heidi Claire!
Heidi Claire who?
Heidi Claire, something
smells delicious!

Knock, Knock!
Who's there?
Emma!
Emma who?
Emma too early for lunch?

Knock, Knock!
Who's there?
Jimmy!
Jimmy who?
Jimmy a chance, and I know I can
make the team!

Knock, Knock!
Who's there?
George!
George who?
George us day, isn't it!

Knock, Knock!
Who's there?
Apple!
Apple who?
Apple your hair if you say no!

Knock, Knock!
Who's there?
Juanita!
Juanita who?
Juanita sandwich with me?

Knock, Knock!
Who's there?
Herman!
Herman who?
Herman grew a moustache
and she hates it!

Knock, Knock!
Who's there?
Polly!
Polly who?
Polly wogs are really
just baby frogs!

Knock, Knock!
Who's there?
Homer!
Homer who!
Homer again after a long day of
school. Time to have some fun!

Knock, Knock!
Who's there?
Jason!
Jason who?
Jason your brother around the house
will get you in trouble!

Knock, Knock!
Who's there?
Wah Zeen!
Wah Zeen who?
Wah Zeen me who broke your
window, honest!

Knock, Knock!
Who's there?
Howell!
Howell who?
Howell I ever get in if you don't
know who I am?

Knock, Knock!
Who's there?
Daisy!
Daisy who?
Daisy goes to school, nights he
plays baseball!

Knock, Knock!
Who's there?
Jerry!
Jerry who?
Jerry funny,
you know very well who it is!

Knock, Knock!
Who's there?
Diane!
Diane who?
Diane to play football, let's go!

Knock, Knock!
Who's there?
Peter!
Peter who?
Peter me, you're just going to have to decide, once and for all, who it's going to be!

Knock, Knock!
Who's there?
Pucker!
Pucker who?
Pucker up, I'm gonna kiss you!

Knock, Knock!
Who's there?
Alfred!
Alfred who?
Alfred I got the wrong door. Sorry!

Knock, Knock!
Who's there!
Dana!
Dana who?
Dana talk to me like that,
young-un!

Knock, Knock!
Who's there?
Sheepritty!
Sheepritty who?
Sheepritty, don't you think?

Knock, Knock!
Who's there?
Deannie!
Deannie who?
Deannie hear me the first time?

Knock, Knock!
Who's there!
Chuck!
Chuck who?
Chuck me the ball and quit asking so
many questions!

Knock, Knock!
Who's there?
Fish!
Fish who?
Fish is temper that dog's got.
He should be on a leash!

Knock, Knock!
Who's there?
Disguise!
Disguise who?
Disguise killing me with these
knock-knock jokes!

Knock, Knock!
Who's there?
Emma!
Emma who?
Emma bugging you yet?

Knock, Knock!
Who's there?
Chair!
Chair who?
Chair you go again,
asking silly questions!

Knock, Knock!
Who's there?
Amy!
Amy who?
Amy 'fraid I may have the wrong
house! You don't look familiar at all!

Knock, Knock!
Who's there?
Discus!
DISCUS who?
Discus throwing inside will
get you detention!

Knock, Knock!
Who's there?
Holly!
Holly who?
Holly cow, Boss, time to head
back to the hide-out!

Knock, Knock!
Who's there?
Doughnut!
Doughnut who?
Doughnut make me reveal my true
identity! I'm undercover!

Knock, Knock!
Who's there?
Patty O.!
Patty O. who?
Patty O'furniture!

Knock, Knock!
Who's there?
Seek!
Seek who?
Seek rat agent. That's a seek rat I
can't tell!

Knock, Knock!
Who's there?
Albany!
Albany who?
Albany of these knock-knock jokes
are there, anyway?

Knock, Knock!
Who's there?
Ray!
Ray who?
Ray member the last time
I was here?

Knock, Knock!
Who's there?
Tommy!
Tommy who?
Tommy you'll always be special!

Knock, Knock!
Who's there?
Glenda!
Glenda who?
Glenda hand! Man, this is heavy!

Knock, Knock!
Who's there?
Dougy!
Dougy who?
Dougy hole in your lawn
by accident! Sorry.

Knock, Knock!
Who's there?
Isabel!
Isabel who?
Isabel out of order? I had to knock!

Knock, Knock!
Who's there?
Alfred
Alfred who?
Alfred the needle if
you tie the knot!

Knock, Knock!
Who's there?
Adolph!
Adolph who?
Adolph ball hit me in de mowf!

Knock, Knock!
Who's there?
Gadget!
Gadget who?
Gadget in your glove, or it'll hit you
in the head!

Knock, Knock!
Who's there?
Arizona!
Arizona who?
Arizona so many times I can knock!

Knock, Knock!
Who's there?
A. Pierre!
A. Pierre who?
A. Pierre at five o'clock,
and you'll find out!

Knock, Knock!
Who's there?
Raymond!
Raymond who?
Raymond me again
what I'm doing here!

Knock, Knock!
Who's there?
Madge!
Madge who?
Madge in my surprise, you're home!

Knock, Knock!
Who's there?
Roberts!
Roberts who?
Roberts are afraid of alarms!

Knock, Knock!
Who's there?
Douglas!
Douglas who?
Douglas is broken, they must have
come in at night!

Knock, Knock!
Who's there?
Greta!
Greta who?
Greta phone, and then
I can stop knocking!

Knock, Knock!
Who's there?
Comb!
Comb who?
Comb down and I'll tell you!

Knock, Knock!
Who's there?
Dwight!
Dwight who?
Dwight when I was gonna
tell you, too.

Knock, Knock!
Who's there?
Eva!
Eva who?
Eva wonder why I always knock?

Knock, Knock!
Who's there?
Bunny!
Bunny who?
Bunny thing is, I know where the
eggs are hidden!

Knock, Knock!
Who's there?
Rabbit!
Rabbit who?
Rabbit around your head
like a turban!

Knock, Knock!
Who's there?
Ron!
Ron who?
Ron house! Sorry! They all look the same!

Knock, Knock!
Who's there?
Sammy!
Sammy who?
Sammy directions next time, and I'll get here faster!

Knock, Knock!
Who's there?
Avenue!
Avenue who?
Avenue heard this joke before!

Knock, Knock!
Who's there?
Santa!
Santa who?
Santa letter telling you I was
coming, didn't you get it?

Knock, Knock!
Who's there?
Moon!
Moon who?
Moon over, and let me
sit on the couch!

Knock, Knock!
Who's there?
Forest!
Forest who?
Forest more than three!

Knock, Knock!
Who's there?
Banana!
Banana who?
Knock, Knock!
Who's there?
Banana!
Banana who?
Knock, Knock!
Who's there?
Banana!
Banana who?
Knock, Knock!
Who's there?
Orange!
Orange who?
Orange ya glad I didn't say banana?

Knock, Knock!
Who's there?
Alvin!
Alvin who?
Alvin a nice time on your porch,
since you ask!

Knock, Knock!
Who's there?
Butcher!
Butcher who?
Butcher money where your mouth is!

Knock, Knock!
Who's there?
Tony!
Tony who?
Tony down in there,
I'm trying to sleep!

Knock, Knock!
Who's there?
Freddy!
Freddy who?
Freddy soon,
you're going to find out!

Knock, Knock!
Who's there?
Butter!
Butter who?
Butter come inside,
it looks like rain!

Knock, Knock!
Who's there?
Evans!
Evans who?
Evans to Betsy, you look tired!

Knock, Knock!
Who's there?
Berlin!
Berlin who?
Berlin hot out here, ain't it?

Knock, Knock!
Who's there?
Moscow!
Moscow who?
Moscows moo but this one
seems very quiet!

Knock, Knock!
Who's there?
Kansas!
Kansas who?
Kansas what tuna comes in, silly!

Knock, Knock!
Who's there?
Boston!
Boston who?
Boston left me in charge of the
whole office for one day!

Knock, Knock!
Who's there?
L.A.!
L.A. who?
L.A. down to take a nap, and I slept
right through dinner!

Knock, Knock!
Who's there?
Gertie!
Gertie who?
Gertie dishes are no fun!

Knock, Knock!
Who's there?
May!
May who?
May my bed for me, would you?

Knock, Knock!
Who's there?
Myron!
Myron who?
Myron is clean! Honest!

Knock, Knock!
Who's there?
Gladys!
Gladys who?
Gladys finally Friday, I can't take
another day of school!

Knock, Knock!
Who's there?
Sadie!
Sadie who?
Sadie magic words, and I'll tell you!

Knock, Knock!
Who's there?
Ida!
Ida who?
Ida done my homework if my dog hadn't eaten it!

Knock, Knock!
Who's there?
Gorilla!
Gorilla who?
Gorilla cheese is good with ketchup!

Knock, Knock!
Who's there?
Eggs!
Eggs who?
Eggs-men are everywhere!

Knock, Knock!
Who's there?
Pizza!
Pizza who?
Pizza me! I'm as surprised as you!

Knock, Knock!
Who's there?
Olive!
Olive who?
Olive the times I've been
to your house!

Knock, Knock!
Who's there?
Sonny!
Sonny who?
Sonny side up please!

Knock, Knock!
Who's there?
Grape!
Grape who?
Grape game the other day. You're still the champ!

Knock, Knock!
Who's there?
Stan!
Stan who?
Stan back, or I'll kick the door down!

Knock, Knock!
Who's there?
Ooze!
Ooze who?
Ooze the boss around here anyway?

Knock, Knock!
Who's there?
Shoe!
Shoe who!
Shoe kid, you're bothering me!

Knock, Knock!
Who's there?
Caesar!
Caesar who?
Caesar before she has time to fill up
her squirtgun!

Knock, Knock!
Who's there?
Julia!
Julia who?
Julia think I'm gonna tell you?

Knock, Knock!
Who's there?
Wylie!
Wylie who?
Wylie answers the door, the bathtub
is overflowing!

Knock, Knock!
Who's there?
Dill!
Dill who?
Dill we meet again, my sweet!

Knock, Knock!
Who's there?
Norma Lee!
Norma Lee who?
Norma Lee I wouldn't come over this late, but can I borrow some milk?

Knock, Knock!
Who's there?
Canvas!
Canvas who?
Canvas be true?

Knock, Knock!
Who's there?
Earl!
Earl who?
Earl gladly tell you if you'd open up!

Knock, Knock!
Who's there?
Terry!
Terry who?
Terry what, why don't you
lend me a dollar?

Knock, Knock!
Who's there?
Cherry!
Cherry who?
Cherry this for me, will you, my
back's killing me!

Knock, Knock!
Who's there?
Epstein!
Epstein who?
Epstein some crazy people,
but you take the cake!

Knock, Knock!
Who's there?
Bat!
Bat who?
Bat you can't wait to find out!

Knock, Knock!
Who's there?
Sparrow!
Sparrow who?
Sparrow couple of quarters, pal?

Knock, Knock!
Who's there?
Lark!
Lark who?
Lark I'm going to tell you!

Knock, Knock!
Who's there?
Goose!
Goose who?
Goose the doctor, you look sick!

Knock, Knock!
Who's there?
Candice!
Candice who?
Candice be any better!

Knock, Knock!
Who's there?
Hardy!
Hardy who?
Hardy recognized you without
your glasses on!

Knock, Knock!
Who's there?
Cows go!
Cows go who?
No they don't, cows go moo!

Knock, Knock!
Who's there?
Ammonia!
Ammonia who?
Ammonia little kid!

Knock, Knock!
Who's there?
Dogs!
Dogs who?
No they don't! Owls hoot!

Knock, Knock!
Who's there?
Mice!
Mice who?
Mice to make your acquaintance!

Knock, Knock!
Who's there?
Rat!
Rat who?
Rat seems to be the problem?

Knock, Knock!
Who's there?
Beaver!
Beaver who?
Beaver quiet and nobody
will find us!

Knock, Knock!
Who's there?
Howzer!
Howzer who?
Howzer day going?

Knock, Knock!
Who's there?
Pitcher!
Pitcher who?
Pitcher eye up to the window and
see for yourself!

Knock, Knock!
Who's there?
Jason!
Jason who?
Jason you all day is
making me tired!

Knock, Knock!
Who's there?
Kenneth!
Kenneth who?
Kenneth the questions or are you
going to talk all day?

Knock, Knock!
Who's there?
Ice Cream!
Ice Cream who?
I scream, you scream, we all scream
for Ice Cream!

Knock, Knock!
Who's there?
Orange juice!
Orange juice who?
Orange juice the guy who
I just talked to?

Knock, Knock!
Who's there?
Antelope!
Antelope who?
Antelope, my parents have already planned the wedding!

Knock, Knock!
Who's there?
Betty!
Betty who?
Betty never guessed it would be me!

Knock, Knock!
Who's there?
Lettuce!
Lettuce who?
Lettuce in, or we'll die of starvation!

Knock, Knock!
Who's there?
Lena!
Lena who?
Lena little closer and maybe
I'll tell you!

Knock, Knock!
Who's there?
Ketchup!
Ketchup who?
Ketchup or you'll get left behind!

Knock, Knock!
Who's there?
Soup!
Soup who?
Souperman to the rescue!

Knock, Knock!
Who's there?
Hi!
Hi who?
Hi who, Hi who,
it's off to work we go!

Knock, Knock!
Who's there?
Woody!
Woody who?
Woody want, can't you see I'm busy!

Knock, Knock!
Who's there?
William!
William who?
William pay attention when
I'm talking to you?

Knock, Knock!
Who's there?
Wayne!
Wayne who?
Wayne, Wayne go away! Come again
some other day!

Knock, Knock!
Who's there?
Funny!
Funny who?
Funny you should ask! I was going
to ask you the same thing!

Knock, Knock!
Who's there?
Iva!
Iva who?
Iva very good idea to tell you!

Knock, Knock!
Who's there?
Hutch!
Hutch who?
You sound like you're coming down
with something!

Knock, Knock!
Who's there?
Owen!
Owen who?
Owen money is no fun!

Knock, Knock!
Who's there?
Answer!
Answer who?
Answer all over your picnic!

Knock, Knock!
Who's there?
Dwayne!
Dwayne who?
Dwayne the bathtub! My bath is finished!

Knock, Knock!
Who's there?
Butter!
Butter who?
Butter up! I'm gonna throw a fast ball!

Knock, Knock!
Who's there?
Arthur!
Arthur who?
Arthur more knock-knock jokes?

Knock, Knock!
Who's there?
Amos!
Amos who?
Amos done reading the
joke book?

Knock, Knock!
Who's there?
Ex!
Ex who?
Ex are great with bacon!

Knock, Knock!
Who's there?
Bacon!
Bacon who?
Bacon from the heat.
It's sweltering out here!

Knock, Knock!
Who's there?
Sonata!
Sonata who?
Sonata as bad as everybody says!

Knock, Knock!
Who's there?
Wendy!
Wendy who?
Wendy you'll remember. Until then,
forget it!

Knock, Knock!
Who's there?
Willy!
Willy who?
Willy ever let you come out?

Knock, Knock!
Who's there?
Yaw!
Yaw who?
Hey, are you a cowboy or what?

Knock, Knock!
Who's there?
Algo!
Algo who?
Algo first as long as you follow right behind!

Knock, Knock!
Who's there?
Darren!
Darren who?
Darren you to read the last page of the knock-knock joke book!

Knock, Knock!
Who's there?
Yachts!
Yachts who?
Yachts a very good question!

Knock, Knock!
Who's there?
Gabe!
Gabe who?
Gabe it my best shot, and that's
all I can do!

Knock, Knock!
Who's there?
Anita!
Anita who?
Anita another knock-knock joke like I
need a hole in the head!